IMMIGRATION, MIGRATION,
AND THE
INDUSTRIAL REVOLUTION

Tracee Sioux

The Rosen Publishing Group's

PowerKids Press
PRIMARY SOURCE

New York

To my grandma, Viola Barksdale, the best cotton-picking woman I know

Published in 2004 by The Rosen Publishing Group, Inc.
29 East 21st Street, New York, NY 10010

First Edition

Editor: Rachel O'Connor
Book Design: Emily Muschinske

Photo Credits: Cover and title page, p. 8 (top) © Corbis, cover and title page (top right) National Museum of American History, Smithsonian Institution; p. 4 (top) © Philadelphia Museum of Art/Corbis; pp. 4 (bottom), 15 (top), 19 (left), 20 © Hulton/Archive/Getty Images; pp. 7 (top, left), 8 (bottom), 12 (top), 15 (bottom), 19 (right) © Bettmann/Corbis; p. 7 (right) Snark/Art Resource, NY; p. 11 Private Collection/The Bridgeman Art Library; 12 (bottom) Ohio Historical Society; p. 16 (top, right) Library of Congress Prints and Photographs Division; p 16 (right) © Underwood & Underwood/Corbis; p. 19 (top) © Michael Maslan Historic Photographs/Corbis.

Sioux, Tracee.
Immigration, migration, and the Industrial Revolution / Tracee Sioux.— 1st ed.
    p. cm. — (Primary sources of immigration and migration in America)
Summary: Describes how inventions such as the cotton gin transformed America from an agricultural country to an industrial one, and led to both problems and opportunities.
Includes bibliographical references (p.   ) and index.
ISBN 0-8239-6826-X (library binding) — ISBN 0-8239-8998-4 (pbk.)
1. Industrial revolution—United States—Juvenile literature. 2. Alien labor—United States—History—Juvenile literature.
3. United States—Emigration and immigration—History—Juvenile literature. 4. Migration, Internal—United States—History—Juvenile literature. [1. Industrial revolution. 2. United States—Emigration and immigration. 3. Migration, Internal.] I. Title. II. Series.
HC105 .S58 2004
330.973'05—dc21
                                    2003000748

Manufactured in the United States of America

Contents

By the late 1800s, America was one of the leading industrial nations in the world. Above: This painting offers a view of what life was like in America before the Industrial Revolution took hold. Left: This image shows factories in Bridgeport, Connecticut, around the 1900s.

4

Changes in America

Before the Industrial Revolution, life in America was mostly centered around land and farming. The U.S. economy depended on agriculture. This meant that drought, frost, floods, or some other natural cause could destroy crops and harm the economy. In the 1800s, the Industrial Revolution, which had begun in Great Britain in the mid-1700s, began to take hold in America. The invention of power supplies, such as steam power and electricity, made the production of goods faster and more efficient. One machine could do the same amount of work as 10 men. America was changing from an economy based on farming to one that was based on industry.

Immigrants Come from Industrial Europe

The Industrial Revolution began in Britain with inventions such as James Hargreaves's spinning jenny and with the improvements James Watt made to the steam engine. It did not create more opportunities and jobs, however. The Industrial Revolution in Britain and the rest of Europe made cities overcrowded and jobs scarce. Many people left Europe to find work in America after the Industrial Revolution had started there. They had heard stories of all the great opportunities in America. From 1840 until 1860, around four million immigrants arrived in the United States from countries such as Britain, Ireland, and Germany.

James Watt (1736–1819) was a Scottish inventor and engineer. This picture shows Watt making improvements to the steam engine in his laboratory.

Right: *The spinning jenny was able to spin 8 to 11 threads at a time.*

Above: *This print, called* Here and There, *tries to show poor families in Europe how life can be better in America.*

Above: African slaves are shown operating one of the first cotton gins, which is short for cotton engine.

Left: Samuel Slater (1768–1835) was born in Britain but is regarded as the founder of America's cotton industry.

The Beginnings of Industrial America

By the end of the 1700s, America was beginning to catch industrial fever. Americans were excited by what machines could do. They offered rewards for scientists in Europe to come to America to help build industrial machines. Samuel Slater, for example, was a British immigrant. He built the first water-powered textile mill in 1790 in Pawtucket, Rhode Island. This was the first real factory in America, and it used machines to spin cotton fibers into yarn. In 1793, a New Englander named Eli Whitney invented the cotton gin, which cleaned cotton by removing its seeds. The invention of these machines and others led to the growth of many factories throughout America.

Migration Within the United States

By the mid-1800s, industrialization really began to take hold, and factories were built in the big cities. People started to migrate from rural parts of America to find work in the cities. The invention of farm machinery, such as the tractor, made farming faster and cheaper than before. Many farmworkers were no longer needed. They had to look for work in steel mills, textile factories, and other industries. These industries were in cities such as New York, Pittsburgh, Boston, or Chicago. For a large number of the jobs in factories, the workers did not need to have many skills.

Opposite: *This is an illustration by Winslow Homer (1836–1910), based on a black-and-white photograph. It is called* Bell Time *and shows many New England factory workers on their way to work.*

Above: *This print shows African Americans (a) in procession from a steamboat landing, (b) setting out for Kansas, (c) eating at a refugee church, and (d) being welcomed to St. Louis.*

Left: *This is a photograph of Walter Black, an African American worker in Ohio in the early 1900s.*

Freed Slaves Move North

Farmers were not the only ones who migrated to America's cities. Many Africans who had been slaves in the South migrated to the North after they were freed in 1865. Some left the South to escape sharecropping because they usually ended up in debt to their former masters. A sharecropper is someone who farms other people's land. He is given credit for things such as seeds, tools, and lodging. At harvest, he receives part of the value of the crop as pay. Some of these earnings are used to repay his credit. Other slaves left the South because of the hostility there toward freed slaves. For example, blacks were persecuted by a group of racist white men called the Ku Klux Klan. Many fled to the North and found work in factories.

Improved Communications

Immigration and migration became easier as the Industrial Revolution progressed. New inventions helped to improve communications and travel. The invention of the steam locomotive in 1804, and the laying of several railroad systems, made migration throughout America much easier. People were able to move from job to job. Also, the invention of the steamship made it quicker and easier for people to emigrate from other countries. The inventions of the telegraph, the telephone, better printing methods, and a good postal service helped to spread the word about job openings and opportunities in new factories.

Right: *The steamship made transport to America a lot quicker than before. Shown is the SS Philadelphia at sea.*

Below: *Alexander Graham Bell invented the telephone in 1876. In this photograph that was taken around the same time, Bell is shown speaking into the first telephone.*

Left: *Here a boy is hard at work at the American Linen Company in Massachusetts.*

Above: *In the Triangle Shirtwaist Fire of 1911, 146 workers were killed because of locked doors and missing fire escapes.*

Poor Working Conditions

The immigrants who arrived in America found work in all kinds of factories. The Industrial Revolution did away with many of the skilled jobs in industry. This created a need for unskilled workers. As a result, jobs in factories were usually boring, repetitive jobs on an assembly line. People often worked for 12 or more hours each day, six days per week. Pay was very low, and working conditions were poor. Factories were often dirty, dark, and unsafe. Child labor was also a problem. It was not uncommon for children as young as five to work in factories. They were paid less than adults, and they were often beaten.

This is a photograph of a young girl in the spinning room at the Globe cotton mill in Augusta, Georgia. It was taken in 1909. It wasn't until 1938 that the Fair Labor Standards Act ended child labor in America.

The Immigrants

Many immigrants in the 1800s were trying to escape a hard life in Europe or in other parts of the world. However, the life that many found in America was also hard. Before 1880, most immigrants came from western and northern European countries, such as Germany, Ireland, Britain, and Sweden. After 1880, as travel and communication grew easier, immigrants came from southern and eastern European countries, such as Italy, Poland, and Greece. From 1866 to 1915, about 25 million immigrants came to America. Many became the factory workers of the Industrial Revolution in the United States.

Bottom Left: *Many immigrants had little money and lived in run-down buildings called tenements. Few immigrants had running water or electricity. This photograph shows immigrants in a tenement building in New York in 1888.*

Right: *Here Italian laborers work on a railway construction project in New York, circa 1900.*

Above: *Shown here are immigrants, possibly Russian, working in a metal shop.*

Immigrant Communities

Each group of immigrants usually went through hard times. They had to deal with persecution, low wages, and sometimes violent treatment before they were accepted by American society. Many of the immigrants tried to keep the traditions of their homelands. They celebrated ethnic holidays, read newspapers in their native language, and ate ethnic foods. They often settled in communities with others from their country. These neighborhoods had names such as Little Italy or Little Poland, after the places from which the immigrants came. Although many immigrants tried to learn English to help them at their jobs, they still spoke their native languages at home.

This photograph from the late 1800s shows the different communities of immigrants as they come together at an outdoor market in New York City.

From Industry to World Power

America was populated by immigrants for whom change was a way of life. This made them open to new ideas and new ways of doing things. This gave America a huge advantage in the Industrial Revolution. In 1851, countries from all over the world gathered to show off their inventions at the first World's Fair in London, England. It became clear that America was ahead of them all. By 1900, the United States had become the leading industrial power, with the richest economy in the world. Most Americans had hoped the Industrial Revolution would help to improve their lives. They never dreamed that such a young nation would reach the heights that it did in such a short period of time.

Glossary

communications (kuh-myoo-nih-KAY-shunz) The sharing of facts or feelings.

credit (KREH-dit) To buy something and promise to pay for it later.

drought (DROWT) A period of dryness that causes harm to crops.

efficient (ih-FIH-shent) Able to do something in the quickest, best way possible.

emigrate (EH-mih-grayt) To leave one's country to settle in another.

ethnic (ETH-nik) Having to do with people of the same race, beliefs, practices, language, or country.

immigrants (IH-muh-grints) People who move to a new country from another country.

Industrial Revolution (in-DUS-tree-ul reh-vuh-LOO-shun) A time in history beginning in the mid-1700s, when power-driven machines were first used to produce goods in large quantities.

locomotive (loh-kuh-MOH-tiv) A train car that pulls the rest of the cars.

migrate (MY-grayt) To move from one place to another.

persecuted (PER-suh-kyoot-ed) Attacked because of one's race or beliefs.

refugee (reh-fyoo-JEE) Having to do with a person who leaves his or her own country to find safety.

rural (RUR-ul) In the country or in a farming area.

textile mill (TEK-styl MIL) A factory where cloth is made.

traditions (truh-DIH-shunz) Ways of doing things that have been passed down over time.

Index

Primary Sources

Cover. *Excelsior Iron Works.* By Lyman W. Atwater. Circa 1870s. **Page 4. Top.** *He That Tilleth His Land Shall Be Satisfied.* Painting. Circa 1850. **Bottom.** Remington Arms Works, Bridgeport, Connecticut. Circa 1900s. **Page 7. Top center.** James Hargreaves's spinning jenny. Circa 1765. **Right.** *Here and There: Or, Emigration a Remedy.* Engraving in *Punch,* London. 1850. **Page 8. Top.** Slaves operate a cotton gin while their owners inspect the finished product. Women carry batches of raw cotton to be cleaned. By William L. Sheppard. Circa 1840–1865. **Page 11.** *Bell Time.* Shows New England factory life. Engraving from *Harper's Weekly.* By Winslow Homer (1836–1910), based on a black- and-white photograph. **Page 12. Top.** African American exodus from the South. Original caption reads: "Remarkable exodus of Negros from Louisiana and Mississippi—Incidents of the arrival, support, and departure of the refugees at St. Louis." Engraving. 1879. **Bottom.** Photograph of Walter Black. 1820. Ohio Historical Center Archives. **Page 15. Top.** The SS *Philadelphia* at sea. Circa 1900. **Bottom.** Original caption reads: "Alexander Graham Bell speaking into the Centennial telephone." Circa 1876. **Page 16. Top center.** A boy, a doffer, standing at a machine. The American Linen Company, Fall River, Massachusetts. Photograph by Lewis Wickes Hine. 1916. **Left.** Fire fighters try to put out the fire, which killed 146 workers as a result of locked doors and missing fire escapes, at the Triangle Shirtwaist Factory in New York. Photograph. 1911. **Right.** A young girl works in the spinning room at the Globe cotton mill in Augusta, Georgia. Photograph by Lewis Wickes Hine. 1909. **Page 19. Top center.** Italian laborers at the New Troy, Rensselaer and Pittsfield Electric Railway, through the Lebanon Valley, New York. Photograph by Michael Maslan. Circa 1900. **Left.** Immigrants in a Bayard Street tenement building. Photograph by Jacob August Riis. 1888. **Right.** Immigrants, possibly of Russian or eastern European origins, working in a metal shop in the United States. A boy stokes a coal-burning stove. Circa 1895. **Page 20.** People inspecting carts filled with fish at an outdoor market at the intersection of Hester Street and Suffolk Street on the Lower East Side, New York City. 1898.

Web Sites

Due to the changing nature of Internet links, PowerKids Press has developed an online list of Web sites related to the subject of this book. This site is updated regularly. Please use this link to access the list:
www.powerkidslinks.com/psima/indust/